GERALD R FORD

ENCYCLOPEDIA of PRESIDENTS

Gerald Ford

Thirty-Eighth President of the United States

By Paul P. Sipiera

Consultant: Charles Abele, Ph.D.
Social Studies Instructor
Chicago Public School System

CHILDREN'S PRESS
A Division of Grolier Publishing
Sherman Turnpike
Danbury, Connecticut 06816

The Ford family in
1975: Seated—Betty and
President Gerald Ford.
Standing—daughter
Susan; sons Steven,
John, and Michael; and
Michael's wife, Gayle

Dedication: For Jill and Owen

Library of Congress Cataloging-in-Publication Data

Sipiera, Paul P.
    Gerald R. Ford / by Paul P. Sipiera.
        p.   cm. — (Encyclopedia of presidents)
    Includes index.
    Summary: Examines the life of the first president to be sworn
into office as a result of his predecessor's resignation.
    ISBN 0-516-01371-8
    1.   Ford, Gerald R., 1913-   —Juvenile literature.
2.   Presidents—United States—Biography—Juvenile literature.
3.   United States—Politics and government—1974-1977—
Juvenile literature.   [1.   Ford, Gerald R., 1913-
2.   Presidents.]   I.   Title.   II.   Series.
E866.S57   1989
973.925'092—dc20   89-33745
[B]   CIP
[92]   AC

Picture Acknowledgments

AP/Wide World Photos, Inc.—4, 6, 8, 15, 16
(bottom), 26, 27, 29 (bottom), 30, 32, 36, 38, 39,
49 (bottom), 50, 52, 58, 63, 64 (2 photos), 68,
69, 70, 71, 74 (2 photos), 78 (2 photos), 79 (2
photos), 80 (2 photos), 81 (top), 84, 89

Courtesy Gerald R. Ford Library—10, 12, 13,
18, 19, 20, 24

UPI/Bettman Newsphotos—5, 9, 16 (top), 17,
23, 29 (top), 33, 34, 35, 41 (2 photos), 44, 48 (2
photos), 49 (top), 54, 57, 65 (2 photos), 66, 75,
81 (bottom), 82, 87 (2 photos), 88

U.S. Bureau of Printing and Engraving—2

Cover design and illustration by
Steven Gaston Dobson

Ford meets with Ronald Reagan at Ford's Rancho Mirage home in California.

Table of Contents

Gerald R. Ford takes the presidential oath of office on August 9, 1974.

Chapter 1

A Tragic End—
A New Beginning

On August 8, 1974, Richard M. Nixon announced his resignation as president of the United States. It marked the end of a long ordeal that had begun some two years earlier. A break-in at the Democratic national headquarters at the Watergate Hotel in Washington, D.C., started investigators on a complex trail of corruption—a trail that eventually led to the White House and forced Nixon's resignation.

No president had ever experienced such disgrace before, and the nation was shocked and angry. The Watergate trials badly undermined people's faith in their government. Not since the assassination of President John F. Kennedy on November 22, 1963, had the nation suffered through such dark days.

Vice-President Agnew defends himself at a press conference.

The job of restoring the country's faith and trust in government fell upon the shoulders of Nixon's vice-president, Gerald R. Ford. Ford had become vice-president through a series of unusual circumstances. Only nine months before, Ford had been the minority leader in the House of Representatives. For the past twenty-five years he had served the state of Michigan as a representative. He was appointed vice-president after the resignation of Spiro T. Agnew, Richard Nixon's running mate in both the 1968 and the 1972 presidential elections. Vice-President Agnew was forced to resign his office after being accused of taking bribes during his term as governor of Maryland. Rather than face a trial, Agnew chose to plead "no contest" (no objection) to a lesser charge of tax evasion.

President Nixon, after much thought, chose Gerald Ford as his new vice-president. He hoped that Ford's reputation for honesty and integrity would restore public

Nixon bids an emotional farewell to his staff and cabinet.

confidence in government and especially in the president's office. The appointment turned out to be short-lived; soon the more dramatic events of Nixon's resignation would thrust Ford into the office of president.

Over the two-and-a-half years that Gerald Ford served as president, he continued to face the challenge of restoring public trust. He had to improve the nation's failing economy and continue peace negotiations with the Soviet Union. He had the difficult task of taking office without having adequate time to prepare. Time was his worst enemy from the start, as the public looked for immediate solutions to very complex problems.

From the perspective of history, the presidency of Gerald R. Ford succeeded in many areas and failed in a few. Perhaps Ford's successor, Jimmy Carter, gave the best description of the Ford presidency when he said it had been "a time to heal."

Chapter 2

Student, Athlete, Politician

The life of the future President Ford seemed destined from the start to be one of change and challenges. Even his name changed before he was five years old. His parents, Dorothy Gardner and Leslie L. King, married in 1912 after a whirlwind courtship. They settled in Omaha, Nebraska, where on July 14, 1913, their son was born. He was named Leslie Lynch King, Jr., after his father. Unfortunately, their marriage did not last, and they were divorced in 1915.

Dorothy King and her son then moved to Grand Rapids, Michigan, to begin a new life. There she met and married Gerald Rudolf Ford in 1916. The marriage turned out to be a happy one, and Mr. Ford formally adopted young Leslie, renaming him Gerald R. Ford, Jr. The boy soon acquired the nickname Jerry. Three more boys, James, Richard, and Thomas, were born in the following years, giving young Jerry three half-brothers. When his natural father remarried, Jerry also gained a half-brother, Leslie, and two half-sisters, Marjorie and Patricia.

Opposite page: Ford in his Grand Rapids
high school football uniform around 1930

Ford at about the age of two

Childhood for young Jerry was a time of fun and learning. His parents were strict but loving. Jerry developed an early interest in sports, fishing, and a variety of outdoor activities. School and church activities were very important to him. Although a stuttering problem caused Jerry some early anxiety, he outgrew it by the age of ten. He did have one unusual characteristic that remained throughout his life—he was both right- and left-handed! Whenever Jerry was sitting down he used his left hand, but when he stood up he used his right hand. Writing left-handed and throwing footballs right-handed upset his parents and

Eagle Scout Jerry Ford (left) with honor guard

teachers, but they failed to change his pattern. All his life, Jerry would change hands as the situation demanded, with no ill effects on him at all. He regarded his unusual trait as quite natural.

Jerry Ford's childhood was much like any other boy's. He and his brothers had their household chores like cutting the lawn and cleaning out the garage. He was taught to abide by the strict moral code observed in his church and community. Occasionally he was caught playing in penny-ante poker games or other forbidden activities and was strictly punished. He participated in the Boy Scouts and earned its highest honor by becoming an Eagle Scout.

In high school Jerry discovered organized sports and the importance of achieving good grades in his studies. In his sophomore year he played center on the city championship football team and was named to the all-city squad. After his junior year, he made the National Honor Society and ranked in the top 5 percent of his class. His best grades came in the subjects of history and government—not surprising, considering his future interests. After school, Jerry waited on tables and washed dishes at a small restaurant across the street from school. He was a hard-working boy in every respect.

In his senior year of high school, Jerry's football team—undefeated in the regular season—went on to win the state championship. The future president captained the all-state squad that year and attracted the attention of many influential people. Jerry also received a scholarship that enabled him to enroll at the University of Michigan in 1931. In later years, Ford would comment that playing football taught him how to be a team player, a lesson that would serve him throughout his life.

University life for Jerry was divided among studies, sports, and part-time jobs. Athletic honors continued to come Jerry's way; he was selected as the outstanding freshman football player of the spring practice. In both his sophomore and junior years, Michigan won the national championship, and Jerry took great pride in the role he played on the team. Senior year found Jerry playing as the starting center, but the team was having a terrible season. Nevertheless, at the end of that season his teammates voted Jerry the most valuable player on the squad.

Ford's experience as a football player enabled him to work off some of his tuition at Yale University as a football coach.

Above: Ford (number 48) as a University of Michigan letterman
Below: Ford at the University of Michigan—most valuable player of 1934

Ford's high school yearbook picture

By the end of his senior year in 1935, Jerry ranked in the upper 25 percent of his graduating class, majoring in both economics and political science. His future prospects looked bright. He even had offers from the Green Bay Packers and the Detroit Lions to play professional football. Although strongly tempted, Jerry felt that professional football was not the way to fulfill his goals. Instead, he decided to look into the study of law. As luck would have it, his athletic ability once again gave him the chance to further his career. After his last season at Michigan, Jerry was offered the position of assistant football coach and freshman boxing coach at Yale University. Jerry had hoped to pursue his law studies at Yale, and now he could earn a living as well by coaching.

Ford (left) with Yale's varsity football staff

At first Jerry Ford divided his time between full-time coaching and part-time law studies. But in 1938, he was accepted into a full-time academic program in law and managed to rank in the upper one-third of his class.

While at Yale Jerry tried his hand at business, at one point entering into a partnership in a New York modeling agency. With his all-American looks, Jerry also became a model for *Look* magazine, appearing in seventeen photo illustrations. Although the modeling agency did well, Jerry eventually decided that the business world was not for him.

Ford at Yale
law school
in 1941

Ford earned his law degree in June 1941 and returned to Michigan for his bar exam. After receiving his license to practice law, he entered into a partnership with Phil Buchen, an old friend from the University of Michigan. While most young lawyers joined established law firms, these two ventured out on their own. Then in December of that year the Japanese attacked the U.S. military base at Pearl Harbor in Hawaii. Suddenly, the United States was at war.

Ford takes a sextant reading on the USS *Monterey*.

Like many other young men in early 1942, Jerry Ford chose to enlist in the U.S. Navy. Because of his university background he was able to enter the service as an ensign. He was sent first to the Naval Academy at Annapolis, Maryland, for basic training and to learn navigation skills. After six weeks, Jerry was transferred to navy flight school at Chapel Hill, North Carolina, where his first duty was as a physical fitness instructor.

Jerry wanted badly to be assigned sea duty on a warship. He kept writing letters to his superiors until they finally assigned him to a light aircraft carrier, the USS *Monterey*. As the ship's athletic director and assistant navigation officer, he served in combat in the Pacific from November 1943 to December 1944.

At one time the *Monterey* was almost lost during a typhoon, when an aircraft broke loose and caused a fire.

Only the brave action of the captain and crew saved the ship. Shortly thereafter, Jerry was transferred to the Naval Reserve Training Command in Glenview, Illinois, for the remainder of the war. It was during this time that Jerry had his closest brush with death. On a mission to Chapel Hill, his plane crashed and he was lucky to escape alive.

In January 1946 Ford was discharged from the navy with the rank of lieutenant commander. Upon his victory ribbon were ten battle stars representing his combat action. His wartime experiences convinced him that America should never again allow its military defenses to weaken. He also realized that America would need strong allies in the future to resist the growing threat of communism. He believed that a revitalized Europe was essential to America's defense and interests. With all his impressions and experiences from the war, Jerry Ford returned to Michigan to resume his legal career.

While most of Gerald Ford's earlier life had been devoted to athletics, academics, and military service, his social life was quieter. In fact, he seemed quite shy at times. He had dated a young woman during his years at Yale, but they parted company when he graduated. Only when he returned to Grand Rapids after the war did he fall in love with the woman who would become his wife. Through the efforts of a mutual friend, Jerry was introduced to Elizabeth (Betty) Bloomer. An attractive fashion coordinator for a local department store, Betty was a former professional dancer with the famous Martha Graham. She and Jerry liked each other immediately and began dating.

At about the same time that he met Betty, Jerry Ford developed an interest in holding a political office. Michigan's Fifth Congressional District congressman Bartel Jonkman was running unopposed for renomination. Jonkman was against all foreign aid to Europe, an issue of particular interest to Jerry. Because no one else wanted to run against Jonkman, Jerry decided to challenge him for the Republican nomination. He had to start in a hurry before Jonkman had a chance to out-campaign him.

By throwing his hat into the political ring, Jerry placed a severe strain on his developing relationship with Betty. Running for office meant spending all his time on the campaign trail. Fortunately for Jerry, Betty was very understanding, and the two shared similar hopes and dreams for their future together. After a two-week separation from each other, Jerry realized how much he missed Betty. When he returned from a campaign trip in February 1948, Gerald Ford proposed marriage to Elizabeth Bloomer. Their wedding on October 15 took place only two weeks before the general election.

The main issue in the race with Congressman Jonkman was foreign policy. Jerry and the incumbent had completely opposite views. Jonkman was against the Marshall Plan to rebuild Europe, and he opposed all other forms of foreign aid. Jerry Ford recognized that the United States needed to help restore the economies of both its allies and its former foes to promote a lasting peace. The Republican primary would prove to be a contest between pre-World War II isolationism and the postwar view of the United States as a world leader in economic and military affairs.

Betty and Jerry leave the church on their wedding day.

When the election results came in, Jerry Ford won a decisive victory over Jonkman by a 2-to-1 margin. It had been a heated and emotional campaign, one that taught Jerry Ford many lessons. The final race against the Democratic candidate proved to be much easier, and Jerry won the seat in the House of Representatives with 61 percent of the vote. The political future of Jerry Ford had been cast, and he would occupy that seat for the next twenty-five years.

Chapter 3

Twenty-Five Years in Congress

In 1948, the year Ford was elected to Congress, the Democrats swept the Republicans out of office in almost every election in the country. Jerry was one of the few new Republicans to take office in 1949. He came to Washington dedicated to the idea that America must retain its position of world leadership. His political philosophy supported the Marshall Plan, a program designed to help Europe recover from the destruction it suffered in World War II. Ford also fought hard for a strong national defense budget and favored a powerful American military presence around the world.

Jerry took his seat in Congress resolved to do the best possible job for his Michigan district and for the country. He quickly realized that he could not do it alone, and he set about hiring the most capable people he could find to serve on his staff. His first and most important appointment was that of John P. Milanowski as his administrative assistant. Together they worked hard to organize an office that would best represent the people who had elected him.

Opposite page: Congressman Ford in 1950

Ford in his Washington, D.C., office as a freshman congressman

As Jerry began his term, destiny seemed to place him among others who would eventually shape American history. One office next to his in the old House Office Building was occupied by a young representative from Massachusetts, John F. Kennedy. On the other side was the office of Thurston B. Morton of Kentucky. Just upstairs was Richard M. Nixon, a second-term representative from California. These men had a great deal in common, and all eventually became powerful figures in government affairs. They had all served in the navy during World War II and shared many wartime stories. Of the three, Jerry became closest to Richard Nixon. They spent time together socially, often discussing their local political issues and

Thurston B. Morton of Kentucky, a fellow congressman

how they would deal with national policy if they had the chance to decide it.

Early in Ford's political career, he made a decision that would guide his actions in Congress over the next twenty-five years. Through the help and advice of John Milanowski, Ford decided to seek the office of Speaker of the House of Representatives. This is a powerful and important position, ranking just under president and vice-president. Although Speaker of the House was a lofty goal for a junior representative to set for himself, Ford felt he could achieve it if he worked hard enough. Jerry never saw the presidency as a goal; he felt he could make his best contributions in the House of Representatives.

During his first two terms in office, Ford maintained a moderate political position, giving equal support to both liberal and conservative issues. In 1952, he had to make several important decisions that would affect his political future. The first was a decision to join seventeen other Republican representatives to urge Dwight D. Eisenhower to run for president. By doing this, Ford established himself as an early supporter of Eisenhower. The second major decision was not to run for a seat in the Senate but to remain in the House of Representatives.

This turned out to be a wise choice. Eisenhower won the 1952 presidential election, and many Republicans were elected at the same time. For the first time in many years, the Republicans held a majority of the seats in Congress.

As Congress returned from its recess in January 1953, Jerry Ford found himself rapidly moving up the political ladder. He was appointed to the defense subcommittee of the House Appropriations Committee and was known for his expertise in military affairs. With a Republican majority in Congress, Eisenhower as president, and his good friend Richard Nixon as vice-president, Jerry felt his future prospects looked good. Yet the nation faced many problems. In his election campaign, Dwight Eisenhower had pledged to bring the Korean War to an end. Even though he helped to settle that conflict, world conditions remained tense. In Russia, Joseph Stalin died, setting off a political power struggle for control of the Soviet Union. Soviet troops were called out to put down a revolt in East Germany, and in faraway Vietnam, the Viet Minh defeated the French military.

Above: Eisenhower after his presidential nomination
Below: Soviet dictator Joseph Stalin in 1946

Senator Joseph McCarthy and his chief counsel, Roy Cohn

At home, Republican senator Joseph McCarthy waged war on communism by accusing numerous government officials and private citizens of being communists. Many people were questioned in hearings and forced to declare their loyalty to the country. Although Jerry Ford was opposed to communism, he did not support the radical activities of McCarthy.

On the personal side, Jerry and Betty Ford enjoyed their life in Washington. Jerry found his time in Congress both challenging and rewarding. Betty enjoyed the Washington life-style while raising their children and maintaining

their home. By now, the Fords had two young sons—
Michael, born in 1950, and John, born in 1952. Two more
children were to arrive in the following years, Steven in
1956 and Susan in 1957.

Yet the strain of being a congressman's wife had its toll.
Betty developed a pinched nerve in her neck that bothered
her all the time Jerry served in Congress. When the condi-
tion did not improve, her doctor, believing the pain may
have been caused by tension and stress, sent her to a psy-
chiatrist for therapy. These visits helped relieve her tensions brought about by the burden of child-raising virtually all alone. Unfortunately, Jerry often had to leave Betty
and the children for long periods of time. Although
devoted to his family, Jerry's political responsibilities
placed a heavy demand on his time. Despite their problems, however, the Fords remained a close and happy
family.

As the 1960s dawned, Ford began to have second
thoughts about his congressional career. He had moved up
to a senior spot on the Appropriations Committee, and his
advice was sought by many. Yet the continual pressure of
campaigning for reelection was taking some of the glitter
out of public office. In addition, his goal of becoming
Speaker of the House seemed more remote since the
Republicans had again lost control of the House. On the
brighter side, Richard Nixon was sure to get the 1960
Republican nomination for president, and there was talk
of Ford becoming his running mate. As it turned out, Nixon chose Henry Cabot Lodge instead. Nevertheless, Jerry
remained loyal and campaigned hard for their election.

President Kennedy announces that the Cuban missile crisis is over.

Democrat John F. Kennedy won the 1960 presidential election by a narrow margin, but the Republicans gained in both the House and Senate. Because of his many years in Congress, Ford was highly respected by members of both parties. His seat on the House Appropriations Committee offered him the opportunity to become the highest-ranking Republican on the defense subcommittee, which controlled the biggest portion of the national budget.

Shortly after Kennedy became president, an American-backed invasion force attempted to overthrow Fidel Castro's government in Cuba. The invasion failed, in large part because the United States did not supply air and naval support. Because Ford knew of the secret invasion plans, he shouldered some of the blame for the operation's

Kennedy inspects military installations in Key West, Florida.

failure. He also later supported Kennedy when Congress tried to cut the president's foreign aid program. Ford's strong stand in favor of the president's position, when most of Congress opposed it, impressed many people.

A second crisis developed in 1962 when an American spy plane found evidence that the Soviets were placing offensive nuclear missiles in Cuba. This was a direct threat to the security of the United States. After the earliest reports of Soviet missiles in Cuba, Ford urged additional spy-plane flights to gather more evidence. These efforts produced the proof that the United States needed, and Russia was forced to remove its missiles. Not until twenty-five years later did Americans learn how close they came to nuclear war during the missile crisis.

Ford after he was voted chairman of the House Republican Conference

In the early 1960s, Ford's popularity increased among the younger Republican members of the House. In 1963, a group of these young representatives known as the Young Turks helped Ford become chairman of the House Republican Conference. This would be Ford's first position of national party leadership, and it gave him his chance to influence Republican policy-making decisions.

Ford's joy over his new position gave way to sadness when John F. Kennedy was assassinated on November 22, 1963. In this senseless act, Jerry lost a cherished friend. Several days later, Ford was appointed to a special commission—known as the Warren Commission—to investigate the Kennedy murder. Based on the findings of this group, Jerry later coauthored a book entitled *Portrait of the*

Johnson takes the presidential oath, flanked by his wife and Jacqueline Kennedy.

Assassin. His book supported the Warren Commission's conclusion that Lee Harvey Oswald had acted alone in killing Kennedy.

Following the assassination, Vice-President Lyndon B. Johnson became president and introduced a flood of legislation dealing with tax cuts, civil rights, Medicare, and other difficult issues. In 1964, campaigning on a promise of what he called the "Great Society," President Johnson ran for another term to continue his programs. Republican Barry Goldwater ran against him but lost the election in November. President Johnson won by one of the largest landslide margins in history, and many Democrats were elected to Congress at the same time. It was a dark time for the Republicans.

Newly-elected House Minority Leader Ford listens to Johnson's State of the Union address.

Just before the 1964 presidential election, a political battle began brewing within the Republican Party. The Young Turks wanted to dump House Minority Leader Charles Halleck in favor of a more progressive-minded person. These political rebels chose Jerry Ford as their best prospect to replace Halleck, because Ford was liked and respected by most of the members of the Republican minority in the House. On January 4, 1965, Jerry won the minority leader's position by a narrow margin of six votes. He held this position until he became vice-president under Richard Nixon in 1973.

By 1965, American involvement in Vietnam had become a serious political issue. Ford had supported President Johnson's early policies on the conduct of the Vietnam War. But as the conflict dragged on, he came out publicly with strong attacks against U.S. military strategy and decision-making policies.

Ford questioned why the United States was not putting its best efforts into the war and urged that the conflict be extended to North Vietnam. In 1967, Ford gave a powerful speech entitled "Why Are We Pulling Our Punches in Vietnam?" It caused many Republicans to oppose President Johnson's war policy. While the battle over Vietnam raged in Congress, the war became increasingly unpopular with the public.

As the 1968 presidential election drew nearer, the Vietnam War began to split the country apart. The Great Society that President Johnson had hoped to create was falling apart, and the president's popularity was dropping fast. Jerry Ford kept up his attacks on Johnson's policies, insisting that America should ensure South Vietnam's independence by winning the war. Ford wanted the government to give U.S. forces in Vietnam the means and direction to win the war instead of remaining on the defensive.

Ford's criticism often provoked angry responses from other congressmen. Republican Senate Minority Leader Everett M. Dirksen of Illinois criticized Ford's opposition to President Johnson's war policy. These two leaders of the Republican Party became embroiled in a minor political war of their own.

A National Guardsman during an urban riot in 1967

Another major issue, civil rights protests, also caused Ford much concern. The urban riots of 1967 in Los Angeles, Detroit, Chicago, and other major cities were tied to the emotion-packed issue of civil rights. Ford's stand against a bill forbidding discrimination in the sale or rental of housing drew much criticism. His work in the House to stop the bill was not effective, and it passed by a comfortable margin. This action was the first real challenge to Ford's leadership, and it hurt to be on the losing side.

As the year progressed, however, the political winds shifted in Jerry Ford's favor. President Johnson chose not to run for reelection, and the presidency seemed wide open for the taking. Jerry Ford looked to the 1968 Republican national convention as an opportunity to demonstrate his

Senate Minority Leader Everett Dirksen of Illinois

political capability. To do that, he needed to be appointed permanent chairman of the convention. This position would give him an excellent base on which to build for future government offices. The appointment proved difficult to get, and Jerry had to ask for the help of his one-time opponent, Senator Dirksen, to ensure his success.

In his opening speech as the convention's chairman, Ford accused President Johnson of "having blundered into a war in Vietnam." He went on to say that "our military strength has dangerously declined" and that "we must rebuild our military power to the point where no aggressor would dare attack us." It was easy to see from his speech that the Vietnam War was going to be a major Republican issue in the November election.

The convention eventually chose Richard M. Nixon as the Republican candidate for president. Jerry Ford, who had hoped Nixon would select him as his running mate, was surprised when Nixon chose Maryland governor Spiro T. Agnew instead. Nevertheless, Ford worked hard for Nixon's campaign. He hoped that a Republican victory would also bring a Republican majority to the House of Representatives. Perhaps then Jerry would be able to realize his dream of becoming Speaker of the House.

Despite all the hard work, Nixon barely won the election, capturing only 43 percent of the popular vote. It was the lowest winning margin since 1912. The Democrats kept control of both the House and the Senate, and Jerry's dream of being Speaker receded once again. Yet all was not lost—after all, an old friend and colleague was president. Perhaps Ford's future was brighter than it appeared.

The nation's future, however, seemed more doubtful. Richard Nixon's new administration inherited many serious problems. The Vietnam conflict was literally out of control, and thousands of Americans were protesting in the streets. Countless young men evaded the military draft, and national spirit was at an all-time low. As more and more American soldiers were killed and wounded in Vietnam, the pressure to end U.S. involvement became greater. Along with the war issue were urban riots, racial clashes, and campus demonstrations. The murders of Martin Luther King, Jr., and Robert F. Kennedy were sad examples of the chaotic events of those times. Something needed to be done quickly to turn things around, or it seemed the country would collapse under its problems.

Above: Funeral procession of Dr. Martin Luther King, Jr., in Atlanta, Georgia
Below: Clutching his rosary beads, Robert Kennedy lies wounded in Los Angeles.

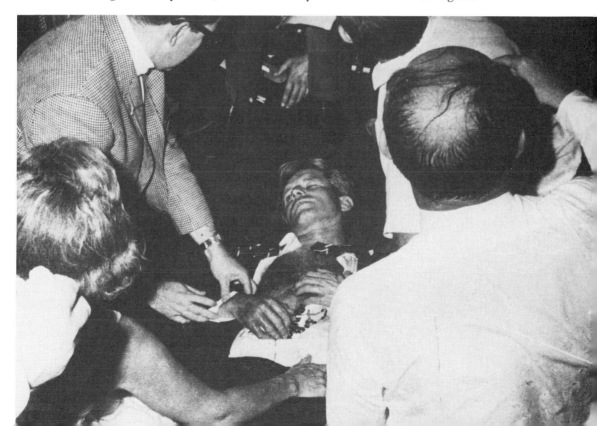

The Nixon presidency did not immediately turn out to be the remedy for America's ills. Richard Nixon ran into trouble with Congress from the start, although Jerry Ford did his best to help out his old friend. Congress and the American public took Ford's efforts in stride and did not condemn him for his actions. Later, it became apparent that Nixon was using Ford to do his political dirty work.

The president also came under constant attack on civil rights issues. Opposition came mainly from black leaders who were angry over Nixon's reluctance to extend the 1965 Voting Rights Act. More than ever, Jerry Ford found himself defending Nixon on a wide range of issues. On many occasions, Ford's loyalty to Nixon seemed to prevail over his own better judgment and over advice from his Republican colleagues in Congress.

The Vietnam issue continued to plague Nixon as it had Lyndon Johnson. Mounting pressure to end the conflict came from all sides. Nixon's official policy toward the war was one of "Vietnamization." This was a program designed gradually to withdraw American troops and to turn over all combat roles to the South Vietnamese army. Ford strongly supported this policy. He also agreed with Nixon that present military actions should be expanded to include bombing North Vietnamese positions in Cambodia. He felt this was the only way to bring the Vietnamese into serious peace talks. When these policies became public, they touched off violent antiwar demonstrations at home and abroad. The worst tragedy took place at Kent State University in Ohio, where four student protesters were killed by National Guard troops. The conduct of the war had turned ugly, and there was even talk of impeaching President Nixon for the illegal bombing of Cambodia.

The year 1971 witnessed several historic events that would affect both national and international affairs. In a bold move, the Nixon administration invited direct diplomatic talks with China and the Soviet Union. These meetings brought new hopes for world peace. On the domestic scene, Nixon imposed a wage and price freeze in an attempt to control inflation. He also imposed an additional tax on imported goods, which angered America's foreign trade partners. This series of bold moves confused Congress, and Jerry Ford had a hard time keeping up with Nixon's ever-changing positions. It became increasingly apparent that Nixon was not informing Congress of his intentions. House and Senate members resented not being consulted about such important matters.

The political situation at home continued to deteriorate. Congress stepped up its attacks on Nixon's Vietnam and economic policies. Nixon was rapidly becoming one of the most unpopular presidents of modern times among members of Congress. He had good reason to worry about his chances for being reelected in 1972. Members of his own party began to side with the Democrats on many issues, and Jerry Ford now spent most of his time simply defending Nixon. Republicans who opposed the president became blacklisted and were regarded by many of Nixon's staff as enemies. At this point Jerry Ford began to wonder if Richard Nixon really knew what was going on within his own political organization. The answer would come soon enough in the wake of the Watergate affair.

Chapter 4

The Watergate Break-In

President Richard Nixon found himself besieged at home over Vietnam and the economic situation. As Jerry Ford worked hard for Nixon in the House, events behind the scenes were undermining all his efforts. Nixon, desperate to win the war, decided to accept a compromise with the Vietnamese. South Vietnam would remain independent, coexisting as a separate state with North Vietnam. To negotiate a cease-fire with North Vietnam, Nixon needed the help of the Soviet Union and China. The price for their cooperation was the political recognition of China, its admission to the United Nations, and a huge grain sale to the Soviets. When details of this settlement leaked out, many conservatives and moderates attacked Nixon and his staff.

Opposite page: Ford and Senator Hugh Scott assure the press that Watergate has not weakened the nation.

45

The president proved equally ill-fated in his response to civil unrest at home. He ordered secret investigations of people and groups in the United States that appeared to pose a threat to national security. This action was provoked by a major student protest demonstration that took place in May 1970.

Nixon's broad directive could easily have been interpreted as an open order to spy on anyone who seemed to be a threat to the government. A small but powerful group of Nixon aides and supporters felt these spy orders should include Nixon's political opponents as well. These aides were greatly concerned about Nixon's reelection, and they planned to do whatever was necessary to ensure a Republican victory in November. Unfortunately, their actions included illegal activities.

This so-called "White House spy network" came to light a few months after June 17, 1972, when a group of men broke into the Democratic Party national headquarters at the Watergate Hotel in Washington, D.C. The burglary operation had been planned by two of Nixon's top aides, E. Howard Hunt and G. Gordon Liddy. By planting hidden microphones in the Democratic offices, they hoped to get information they could use to help Nixon with the presidential election.

When news of the break-in became public so close to the election, a cover-up began. Nixon and his staff hoped to downplay the Watergate break-in until after the November election. This would give Nixon the time he needed to end the Vietnam War. If he succeeded, then his place in history would be assured.

Public reaction to Watergate was at first rather subdued. The press reported the event but did not press the issue of who was responsible. Occasionally someone would bring up the question and ask Nixon if he knew who was behind the break-in. His basic response was that such actions had "no place whatever in our electoral process [and] the White House has had no involvement whatever in the particular incident."

The public believed Nixon, and so did Jerry Ford. At the time, Ford could not have known that the five men arrested for the break-in were part of a political spy scheme rooted in the White House. The Democrats were eager to keep the issue alive and tried to use it in the campaign. As election day drew near, however, Watergate had all but faded from public view.

The 1972 election returned Richard Nixon to the White House with an impressive victory. Jerry Ford, too, easily won reelection to the House; but once again the Republican Party had failed to get control of either the House or the Senate. Without a majority in the House, Jerry had to give up his dream of becoming Speaker of the House. This latest setback made him think about leaving Congress and returning to private life. In early 1973, Jerry decided to seek one more term of office and then retire in January 1977.

As Nixon was sworn in for his second term, things began to change rapidly. Watergate was not going away, as the president had hoped. The Senate created a special committee, headed by Sam Ervin of North Carolina, to look into the Watergate break-in.

**Above: Former CIA spy E. Howard Hunt
Below: Nixon aide G. Gordon Liddy**

Above: Senator Sam Ervin, Senate Watergate Committee chairman
Below: Removing furniture from the vacated Democratic headquarters

Nixon announces that he will turn over transcripts of White House tapes.

In a mid-April speech before a gathering of Michigan Republicans, Ford challenged all administration officials accused of being involved in Watergate to "go before the Senate committee" and "take an oath and deny [their involvement] publicly." Nixon, who had up to now refused to let his aides testify, gave in. The president wanted to exercise his right of "executive privilege" to keep some of the testimony secret, but this was not granted. However, he was given the courtesy of having his own legal representative present at the hearings. Jerry Ford was pleased with this outcome, and he won praise from both the House and the Senate for his part in it.

As April passed, more and more evidence pointed to Nixon's active role in the Watergate conspiracy. During the hearings, a sudden rush of disclosures erupted from the witnesses. Those involved in Watergate began to tell all they knew in an effort to save themselves from criminal prosecution and possible jail sentences. It also came to light that some witnesses had lied and that their superiors were trying to hide the truth. Government aides resigned or were dismissed at a dizzying pace. The hand of justice was reaching deeper into the ranks of the Nixon administration, and many important jobs were now vacant. People began to wonder just how far up into the government the corruption reached. It was becoming difficult for the office of the president to function at all.

Jerry Ford, who still believed completely in Richard Nixon's innocence, worried about how these vacancies would affect the daily operations of the White House. In an effort to help out, Jerry began asking his old political friends and allies to rally around the president and help him maintain a functioning administration. Jerry believed in Nixon's innocence and he felt that the administration would survive. He believed that faith and trust in the government could be restored once the "bad apples," the corrupt aides, were removed.

Throughout the Watergate affair, Ford stood by Nixon, voting with the president's positions 83 percent of the time. It was a strong record of support and clearly showed Ford's deep trust in Nixon. Because he had no idea how deeply Nixon was involved in Watergate, the events that followed caught Ford totally by surprise.

Chapter 5

Good-Bye, Congress—
Hello, Mr. Vice-President

As 1973 wore on, the Watergate investigations continued to astonish the American public. Criminal trial proceedings against some of the defendants began, while the Nixon administration tried to restore a sense of "business as usual" to the White House. Toward the end of the year, yet another crisis struck that would thrust Ford from the House into the vice-presidency. On October 10, Vice-President Spiro Agnew was forced to resign his office under threat of criminal prosecution for taking bribes. Thus Agnew became only the second vice-president in U.S. history, after John C. Calhoun in 1832, to resign his office.

The Twenty-Fifth Amendment to the Constitution, just passed in 1967, provides instructions for filling a vacancy in the vice-presidency. The president is to nominate a candidate, and both houses of Congress are to approve the nominee by a majority vote.

Opposite page: Vice-President Ford, 1974

Vice-President Agnew announces his resignation.

Shortly after Agnew's resignation, President Nixon called a conference of congressmen, state governors, and Republican national committeemen to help select a replacement for Agnew. The special conference took only two days to recommend Gerald Ford as Agnew's successor. President Nixon then nominated Ford as the new vice-president, subject to Congress's approval.

Ford had not been Nixon's first choice. On the list ahead of Ford were John Connally, Nelson Rockefeller, and Ronald Reagan. Nixon was persuaded to choose Ford largely on the advice of his advisers Alexander Haig and Melvin Laird. They believed it would be nearly impossible to get the unpopular Connally confirmed by Congress. As for

Rockefeller and Reagan, their selection might split the Republican Party between moderates and conservatives. Ford remained the one candidate most likely to be both confirmed by Congress and approved by the party.

The nomination of Jerry Ford as successor to Spiro Agnew came as a relief. Now his appointment had to pass the approval of the Senate and the House. In light of the scandal brought about by Agnew's resignation, everyone wanted to make sure Ford's background was clear. The investigation began with an FBI check into Ford's life. Next, his income tax returns since 1965 were examined. Then the Library of Congress conducted a complete review of Ford's political stand on every issue on which he had voted for the past twenty-five years. Before it was all over, Jerry Ford had laid his entire life before the public. Never before had such extensive measures been taken, but Congress wanted to be sure of the man they confirmed as vice-president.

In his nationally televised appearance before the Senate Rules and Administration Committee, Ford was asked many challenging questions. His answers to queries about executive privilege, impoundment of congressionally appropriated funds, and the appointment of a new Watergate prosecutor received the most scrutiny. In defense of his nomination, Ford pointed out that his many years of service in the House had given him the experience he needed to be a good vice-president. He also declared that, if confirmed as vice-president, he did not plan to run for president in 1976. He did not want to be accused of using the present situation to help him become president.

When asked about his personal political philosophy, Ford replied: "Moderate in domestic affairs, conservative in fiscal affairs, and dyed-in-the-wool internationalist in foreign affairs." National security was his top spending priority. In these statements, Jerry Ford spoke frankly about his deepest beliefs.

Ford's honesty and openness during the confirmation hearings impressed many people. The only black mark that turned up from the many investigations involved charges made by a lobbyist named Richard N. Winter-Berger. Winter-Berger claimed that Ford granted special favors for campaign contributions and took $15,000 in cash payments. He also stated that Ford received treatment for depression and a nervous condition that resulted from the pressures of being a congressman. All of these charges were later dismissed for lack of proof.

The Senate committee indicated that they viewed Ford more as a potential president than simply as a vice-president. After three days of public hearings, nine closed sessions, and perhaps the most detailed FBI investigation ever made of a candidate for public office, they concluded that they found nothing to disqualify Ford from the vice-presidency. On November 27, 1973, the Senate approved Gerald Ford's nomination by a 92-to-3 vote.

Next came confirmation by the House of Representatives. First the hearings focused on one basic question: Should they even consider the nomination of a vice-presidential candidate from a president who was himself under threat of impeachment? Debate raged for several days, and Ford had to support his own cause by pledging "to be

Ford and House colleagues after his confirmation as vice-president

his own man" and tell the president when he was wrong. Ford also stated that his twenty-five years in Congress were "fine training" for the presidency, if he should be called upon to assume that office.

In the end, the committee went on record with the statement: "Looking at the total record, the committee finds Mr. Ford fit and qualified to hold the high office for which he has been nominated pursuant to the Twenty-fifth Amendment." On December 6, 1973, the House approved Gerald R. Ford's nomination as the nation's vice-president, by a vote of 387 to 35. All thirty-five dissenting votes were cast by Democrats.

This marked the first time in American history that a vice-president had been chosen under the guidelines of the Twenty-Fifth Amendment to the Constitution. For Gerald Ford and for the nation, his appointment was truly a historic event.

Chapter 6

Vice-President Gerald R. Ford

Within an hour after the House of Representatives approved his nomination on December 6, 1973, Gerald R. Ford was sworn in as the nation's new vice-president. Before a joint session of Congress, Ford took the oath of office from Chief Justice Warren E. Burger. Betty Ford held the Bible upon which Jerry took the oath, with a smiling President Nixon looking on. A definite air of excitement surrounded the occasion, and President Nixon had a White House celebration for Ford after the formalities were over. In his acceptance speech, Jerry joked that he was "a Ford, not a Lincoln," and promised to do the best job possible in his new office.

With all the trials of the confirmation hearings behind him, Jerry Ford assumed his duties as vice-president. One of the more visible responsibilities of the office is to be the presiding officer in the Senate. In Jerry's first appearance before that body, he proclaimed that he would stand for "the rule of law and equal justice." His only promise was "to do the very best job I can for America." It would be a bright beginning as he left behind his twenty-five years in the House of Representatives and assumed his new position next to the president.

Outside the White House, however, public opinion was turning against Nixon. More people within and outside Washington were calling for Nixon to resign or for impeachment proceedings to begin. Jerry Ford's most important job would be to restore public confidence in the White House. This proved to be a difficult task.

Ford's early expectations that he and Nixon would be an effective team faded quickly. President Nixon was beginning to feel the strain of the Watergate investigations. He withdrew into a protective shell and let most of the responsibility for running the government fall to White House Chief of Staff Alexander Haig and Secretary of State Henry Kissinger. Ford, on the other hand, took on numerous speaking engagements in which he tried to keep the Republican Party's morale high and to defend the president's position. This approach began to cause Jerry trouble. It gave the impression that he was not following his own beliefs but merely repeating words given to him by the president's speech writers.

As Ford's speaking engagements attracted attention, the troubled situation at the White House bothered him more and more. His speeches reflected his own growing conflict over Nixon. One day Ford would speak out in defense of the president, and the next day he would deliver a speech critical of Nixon's actions. His speeches appeared to fuel the controversy instead of resolve it. Yet he was trying to place himself between the president and Congress, hoping to find a compromise that would satisfy both sides. He did not succeed. In fact, through this awkward approach, he confused people about his own position.

Yet Ford resisted those who advised him to keep quiet. He continued his public expression of loyalty to President Nixon. But he also started privately pressuring the White House to release evidence that would bring the Watergate affair to a conclusion. Unfortunately, Ford's talks with White House aides proved useless. He began to suspect that he was being used to buy more time for Nixon. White House staffers appeared to be less interested in providing evidence and more interested in preparing Nixon's defense for a possible impeachment trial. At that point, Ford felt that he no longer had any influence in the White House or with Richard Nixon.

One of the biggest controversies in the Watergate investigations arose over tapes of recorded conversations between the president and those involved in the cover-up. These tapes were considered vital evidence, but the White House refused to release them for the trial proceedings. At first, Jerry Ford turned down an offer to hear the tapes. Later, when he did listen to them, he stated publicly that they could be interpreted in different ways. But he had heard enough to seriously question the innocence of Richard Nixon. Jerry's faith and trust in his longtime friend had been shaken—could he ever again be sure if Nixon was lying or telling the truth?

Unknown to Jerry Ford, his old law partner Philip Buchen, now Ford's personal adviser, was secretly putting together a presidential transition team in the event that Nixon resigned or was impeached. If Jerry Ford were to become president, he would have to have some organization in place or the transition could be a disaster. Buchen kept his work secret even from Jerry. Had Ford known of these activities, he would have stopped them, believing they would hurt the president's position even more. When asked by the press about the existence of such a transition team, Ford honestly denied any knowledge of it. When he was later called upon to become president, however, he was grateful to discover the team existed.

The turning point in the Watergate investigations came on July 24, 1974, when the Supreme Court ordered President Nixon to turn over his Watergate tapes to the special prosecutor. Nixon no longer had a choice in the matter, and he handed over the tapes. Controversy broke out over the now-famous "missing eighteen minutes" on one tape and erased sections of other tapes. The tapes demonstrated that Nixon was involved in an active cover-up scheme as early as six days after the Watergate break-in.

At this time, Ford was still publicly defending the president's innocence in his speeches. When word came that Nixon might resign or be impeached soon, Jerry toned down his defense of the president. Nixon continued to give people the impression that he would fight to the bitter end. This attitude amazed and dismayed everyone close to him.

The next few days were hectic in the White House. Nixon's aides prepared for a long and difficult impeachment trial while trying to maintain a functioning government. Jerry Ford's staff, on the other hand, labored hard on a plan to make the transition from Nixon to Ford as smooth as possible. Jerry was now being kept informed on all matters as if he were already the president. All over the nation and the world, people anxiously awaited news from the

Nixon bids a tearful farewell to his White House staff.

White House. A decision was finally made on the evening of August 7, when Richard Nixon told his family that he intended to resign as president. Then he informed his White House staff. Finally Nixon seemed to be at peace with himself. The long ordeal was over!

President Nixon met with Jerry Ford late that evening and told him of his plans for resigning. For the next hour and ten minutes they talked, and Jerry offered words of sympathy. They discussed arrangements for the next day and outlined Nixon's public resignation on national television. They agreed that, before addressing the nation, Nixon would meet with his White House staff and their families to express his personal regrets and to thank them for their loyalty and support. Just before his letter of resignation was delivered to Secretary of State Kissinger, Nixon would leave for his home in California. Within two days, Jerry Ford would be the new president.

Above: Judge John Sirica, who ordered Nixon to release his tapes
Below: Members of the Senate Watergate Committee

Above: White House counsel John Dean and his wife, Maureen
Below: Senators Percy and Pell review a list of White House tapes.

Chapter 7

President Ford:
A New Beginning

On August 9, 1974, at three minutes past noon, Gerald R. Ford, Jr., became the thirty-eighth president of the United States. He was the first to hold that office without having been elected president or vice-president. Ford's swearing-in ceremony would be different from those of his predecessors. It was not a time for celebration but a time for picking up the pieces of a fallen administration. Ford did not intend to sit back quietly for the next two-and-a-half years and enjoy the White House. He was determined to do all he could to get the country back on its feet and to restore pride and trust in the government.

The many problems facing Jerry Ford would test his abilities to the limit. His first challenge was to rebuild the cabinet and the White House staff. Ford asked most of the Nixon cabinet to remain in their posts and requested their help and cooperation. One of the most important positions was that of the White House chief of staff. Much to Jerry Ford's delight, Alexander Haig assured him that he would remain in that post.

Ford and Governor Nelson A. Rockefeller

Ford moved at a hectic pace during his first ten days in office. He sent personal messages to all the world's leaders assuring them that America's foreign policy and worldwide commitments would remain the same as they were in the Nixon administration. Slowly the functions of government were returning to normal, and the public responded with genuine support for Jerry Ford.

Soon after taking office, Ford nominated Governor Nelson A. Rockefeller of New York to fill the vacant vice-presidency. While the choice came as no surprise, Ford's next announcement surprised everyone. He announced that he would "probably" run for president in 1976. His decision caught people off guard, particularly since Ford had promised during his confirmation hearings for vice-

Turkish paratroopers after landing in Cyprus

president that he would not run for the presidency in
1976. Perhaps his first two weeks in office convinced him
that being president was what he wanted after all.

Once the White House staffing was completed, Ford
started tackling the problems at hand. On the international
scene, a 1973 war in the Middle East, between Egypt and
Israel, had subsided under an uneasy truce that could be
broken at any moment. In August, Turkish troops invaded
the Mediterranean island of Cyprus. Although the United
States was not involved, it was being blamed for not pre-
venting the invasion. The conflict was a sensitive issue in
the United States because it affected many Greek-
Americans. These were only the first of many challenges
Jerry Ford would have to face in international relations.

Ford announces his "full, free and absolute pardon" of Nixon.

Ford was no stranger to controversy on the domestic scene, either. Although at first Congress treated the new president with a certain warmth, the "honeymoon" did not last long. The first major conflict came soon after Ford assumed office. In a single, bold move, Jerry Ford went on national television and pardoned Richard Nixon for all federal crimes he may have committed as president. This action shocked the country and severely hurt Ford's popularity. Even Ford's close friend and press secretary, Jerry terHorst, resigned his position in protest over Nixon's pardon.

Why did Ford pardon Nixon so soon after taking office? The reasons are complex. Both the press and the public had been demanding action against Nixon for his involve-

Press Secretary Jerald terHorst

ment in Watergate. President Ford was asked what was going to happen to Nixon at every press conference, and he felt the issue was drawing attention away from more pressing matters. Also, Nixon was in poor health at the time. Ford had visited Nixon in the hospital and was shocked by his physical appearance. The pressures from Watergate and the resignation were taking their toll. Jerry felt that, if Nixon knew he would not have to deal with a possible trial and prison sentence, his health would improve. Ford also considered how much time a trial would take. The best estimates were from nine months to two years. Ford was convinced that a long trial would not be in the country's best interests, and the time could be better spent on more constructive matters.

Soon after he pardoned Nixon, Jerry Ford offered amnesty to all draft dodgers and deserters of the Vietnam War. This decision also proved controversial. War veterans' groups were generally opposed to the offer, while the public was more accepting. Most people just wanted the war and all reminders of it to fade quickly and quietly. Ford's offer carried a few conditions, however. Those who chose to accept it were required to do public service for up to two years. The program was only some-what successful. Of the 106,000 men eligible, only 22,000 ever applied for it.

Ford also inherited serious economic problems from the Nixon administration. Inflation—rapidly rising prices— threatened to spiral out of control. Ford fought back by establishing a Council on Wage and Price Stability. This council reported any wage and price increases in the coun-try that went higher than limits set by the government. If inflation was to be controlled, the entire country had to pull together.

One way to hold prices down was to increase taxes, but the economy suffered a setback, called a recession, before those plans could be put into effect. Another approach was to create new public service jobs and actually *lower* taxes. This plan was introduced and passed by Congress. By early 1975, the economy did show signs of recovery and infla-tion slowed, with unemployment dropping slightly from its earlier record high. Things were improving just a bit, and Jerry was encouraged.

One of the bright spots in the former Nixon administra-tion had been in the area of foreign policy. Jerry Ford inherited a capable, if controversial, secretary of state, Henry Kissinger. With his help and advice, Ford handled the evacuation of U.S. military and civilian personnel from South Vietnam as the war drew to an end. In addition, difficult negotiations were under way between Egypt and Israel, with hopes for peace in the Middle East hanging in the balance. Finally, Nixon's visit to China had opened the door to further cooperation between the United States, Russia, and the People's Republic of China. Any one of these issues would have been challenging, and Ford had to handle all three.

Perhaps the most difficult problem facing Jerry Ford was the fall of South Vietnam and the hordes of refugees fleeing that country. Back in 1973, the United States had agreed to pull out most of its troops as part of the Paris Peace Accords. The North Vietnamese promised not to invade South Vietnam as their part of the agreement, but they did not keep their pledge for long. Without U.S. troop support and financial aid, South Vietnam could not defend itself.

By January 1975 the North Vietnamese had captured the first southern province, and by March, had gained twelve more. The end of South Vietnam was near, and not even last-minute U.S. aid could save it. By the end of April 1975, Saigon, the capital of South Vietnam, had fallen and the war was over. America's reputation had been severely damaged by the long, bloody conflict. America's allies questioned U.S. commitments and wondered what kind of stand the United States would take against communism in the future.

Above: Dien Bien Phu, whose fall divided Vietnam in 1954
Below: Ford, Kissinger, and Army Chief of Staff Frederick Weyand

Evacuees file into a helicopter on a rooftop in Saigon, South Vietnam.

The fall of Vietnam, however, was not the end of America's involvement in Southeast Asia. The United States was challenged almost immediately by the Khmer Rouge forces that had just taken over Cambodia (now renamed Kampuchea). As America's allies were questioning the nation's commitments, a Cambodian naval vessel seized an American merchant ship, the SS *Mayaguez*, in international waters. No one knew whether this was an act of war or piracy, but Ford had to decide on quick action. He was concerned for the safety of the thirty-nine crewmen on board the ship. But since no official government existed in Cambodia, negotiations were not possible. A military operation seemed to be the only choice.

The president approved a military rescue under the authority granted him by the War Powers Act. After informing Congress of his plans, Ford gave the go-ahead and the operation began. A Marine invasion force rescued the ship and its crew after Cambodian officials announced their willingness to comply with U.S. demands. The price for the rescue was high; 41 Americans were killed and 50 wounded. The number of casualties disturbed President Ford greatly. He felt that the operation had not been carried out effectively. Although the mission succeeded and showed the world America's willingness to fight, Ford regretted that it had to cost so many lives in the process.

In international diplomacy, Ford continued the work begun by Richard Nixon. Before Nixon left office, he had agreed to a state visit to Japan. He would have been the first U.S. president to visit that country. Jerry Ford honored his commitment in November 1974. While in Japan, he discussed many matters of concern to both countries and left with a better understanding of Japan's economic and defense issues. Ford then traveled to South Korea to meet with its president and visit U.S. troops stationed there.

The third stop on his Far Eastern tour took him to an informal meeting with Soviet president Leonid Brezhnev in Vladivostok. This important meeting set the groundwork for a treaty designed to reduce the number of nuclear weapons and the threat of war. The meeting also helped to thaw the Cold War between East and West. It eventually led to a symbolic joint U.S.-U.S.S.R. manned space mission in 1975.

Jerry Ford's first year in office had been a success overall. He attacked the nation's economic problems, and they seemed to be slowly improving as a result of his efforts. The Vietnam War was over, and the wounds from that conflict had begun to heal. Negotiations with the Soviets were progressing well, raising people's hopes for peace. Even Watergate was fading from the public eye. Then, in the midst of Ford's success, tragedy almost struck.

On September 5, a twenty-six-year-old woman named Lynette Alice Fromme tried to kill the president. Breaking out of a crowd as Ford walked by, she pointed a pistol directly at him but was grabbed by Secret Service agents before she could fire. Fromme was later convicted and sentenced to life imprisonment for her attempt on Ford's life. Less than three weeks later the scene was repeated. Another young woman, Sara Jane Moore, fired a pistol at the president, narrowly missing him. The president's life was saved by a former Marine Corp veteran, Oliver Sipple. Sipple, who saw Moore point the pistol, struck her hand as she fired, and the bullet missed its mark. She, too, was convicted and sentenced to life imprisonment. Despite these frightening experiences, Ford refused to cancel future public appearances.

The Ford presidency was going well as the nation looked forward to the bicentennial celebration of America's two hundred years of independence. Jerry Ford, despite his promise not to run for president, decided to enter the 1976 election campaign. He felt that his administration was doing a good job and that, given four more years, he could make a significant contribution to the country.

President Ford makes a state visit to Seoul, South Korea, in 1974.
Above: Confetti rains on his motorcade. Below: With President Park Chung-Hee

Above: Ford and Japanese emperor Hirohito
Below: Ford with Soviet leader Leonid Brezhnev

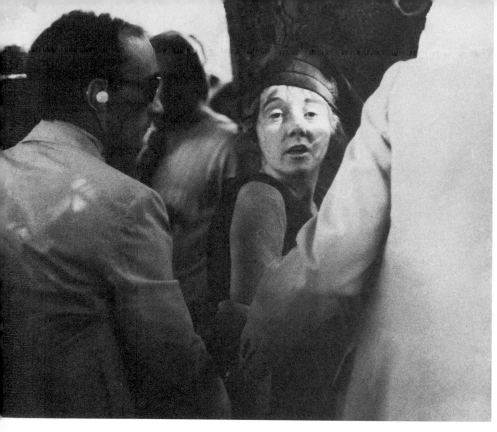

Above: Lynette Fromme after her assassination attempt
Below: Secret Service agents shield Ford from Lynette Fromme.

Above: In San Francisco, Ford ducks after Sara Jane Moore has fired.
Below: Sara Jane Moore, who escaped from federal prison and was recaptured

Ford with running mate Robert Dole at the Republican convention

The election would not be easy. Ford did not have a strong campaign organization behind him, as did other Republican candidates at this time. The most serious challenge for the Republican nomination came from former governor Ronald Reagan of California. Ford and Reagan fought a close and often bitter contest in the state primaries. At the Republican national convention, Jerry Ford won a narrow victory over Reagan on the first ballot. Senator Robert J. Dole of Kansas was chosen as his running mate instead of Vice-President Nelson Rockefeller. Ford and Dole would face former governor James E. Carter, Jr., of Georgia and Walter Mondale of Minnesota in the November election.

The 1976 election proved to be a close race. Jerry Ford had campaigned on the basis of his administration's successful record. He promised to continue the policies that had brought about improved international relations, economic recovery, and lower inflation.

For his part, Carter charged that Ford was actually mismanaging the economy and would bring about economic ruin. Carter cited the high rate of unemployment as an example. The Democratic candidate's attacks were effective and put Ford on the defensive. Carter also brought up Watergate and Ford's pardon of Nixon. His speeches gave many people a bad impression of Jerry Ford's handling of the entire affair.

Carter won the election by a narrow margin. After a long night in which the lead swung back and forth between Carter and Ford, Jerry finally conceded victory to his opponent the next morning. The two were separated by only 1,678,069 votes out of over 81.5 million cast. Ford won 27 states to Carter's 23, but Carter won the electoral vote, 297 to 240. The campaign was over for Jerry Ford. The defeat was hard to accept, since he had never lost an election in his twenty-five years of campaigning. It may be that Ford lost not for lack of ability or accomplishments, but because the scars of Watergate were simply too deep. The country wanted a fresh start, and they chose Carter to lead the way.

Jerry Ford left the White House with dignity and pride in the fact that he had done the best job he could. And indeed, the country was fortunate to have had him in the White House at a time when such a man was needed most.

Chapter 8

Life after the Presidency

At the close of the second century of American democracy, Jerry Ford had helped to heal the wounds of the nation. As the third century began, Ford was on the scene long enough to get it started in the right direction. On January 20, 1977, he left the White House for the last time as president. Jimmy Carter was sworn in as the thirty-ninth president that same day, and he expressed his hopes that he could continue the progress made by Gerald Ford. Although it was hard to leave office, Ford left behind an excellent record of public service that spanned over twenty-eight years. He had served proudly in the House of Representatives and worked hard throughout the short time he was vice-president. As president, Ford gave back to the country a sense of pride and trust in the government. The future for the United States looked brighter than it had in a long time.

Opposite page: Former president Ford golfs in the Bob Hope Desert Classic tournament.

85

Perhaps the best job in the world is that of being an ex-president of the United States. The responsibilities of the presidency are gone, but the respect and prestige remain. After leaving office, Jerry and Betty Ford retired to southern California to enjoy the relaxation they deserved. Retirement would finally give Jerry Ford time to enjoy his favorite recreational pastimes, golf and skiing. A long-time avid golfer, Jerry loved the year-round warm climate that let him indulge in endless rounds of the sport. He often participated in charity golf events to help raise funds for worthy causes.

Both Jerry and Betty Ford donated their time and energies to many charitable organizations. One in particular was the establishment of the Betty Ford Foundation to help people overcome drug and alcohol abuse problems. Over the years this institution has helped many people return to a normal life free of these terrible dependencies. The Fords also made public appearances to establish and support the Gerald R. Ford Museum in Grand Rapids and the Gerald R. Ford Library in Ann Arbor, Michigan. Both institutions were founded to give scholars access to documents on Ford's background and on his presidency.

Jerry Ford's involvement in politics did not end with his retirement. In election years Jerry made many appearances in support of fellow Republicans running for office, and they often sought his opinions and advice. During Ronald Reagan's administration in the 1980s, Jerry was asked to carry out several important assignments for the president. Ford always remained available to his successors to give advice and cooperation whenever the need arose.

Above: Betty and Jerry leave Washington, D.C., as private citizens.
Below: Ford and President Reagan after a breakfast meeting in 1982

The Fords appearing on the Donahue Show in Chicago

Life after the presidency for Jerry Ford may have been less pressured, but he remained as active as ever. He continued to serve on the board of directors of several companies and to give many public lectures as well. He was in high demand as a speaker for colleges, universities, and various organizations, and his fees made his retirement years quite comfortable. In 1979, Jerry found time to write his autobiography, entitled *A Time to Heal*. The book gave him an opportunity to share his views on his life and political career.

The Fords before his speech at the 1984 Republican convention

As president, Gerald Ford's greatest accomplishment was that he held the country together at a time when it was splitting apart. He inherited a government wounded by its own corruption, and he guided it through a time of healing. Perhaps Ford would not have been the people's first choice to deal with the circumstances of the time. But perhaps no one could have done a better job than he did. He proved that the American system of democracy does work. If for this achievement alone, the nation can take pride in his presidency.

Chronology of American History

(Shaded area covers events in Gerald Ford's lifetime.)

About A.D. 982—Eric the Red, born in Norway, reaches Greenland in one of the first European voyages to North America.

About 1000—Leif Ericson (Eric the Red's son) leads what is thought to be the first European expedition to mainland North America; Leif probably lands in Canada.

1492—Christopher Columbus, seeking a sea route from Spain to the Far East, discovers the New World.

1497—John Cabot reaches Canada in the first English voyage to North America.

1513—Ponce de Léon explores Florida in search of the fabled Fountain of Youth.

1519-1521—Hernando Cortés of Spain conquers Mexico.

1534—French explorers led by Jacques Cartier enter the Gulf of St. Lawrence in Canada.

1540—Spanish explorer Francisco Coronado begins exploring the American Southwest, seeking the riches of the mythical Seven Cities of Cibola.

1565—St. Augustine, Florida, the first permanent European town in what is now the United States, is founded by the Spanish.

1607—Jamestown, Virginia, is founded, the first permanent English town in the present-day U.S.

1608—Frenchman Samuel de Champlain founds the village of Quebec, Canada.

1609—Henry Hudson explores the eastern coast of present-day U.S. for the Netherlands; the Dutch then claim parts of New York, New Jersey, Delaware, and Connecticut and name the area New Netherland.

1619—The English colonies' first shipment of black slaves arrives in Jamestown.

1620—English Pilgrims found Massachusetts' first permanent town at Plymouth.

1621—Massachusetts Pilgrims and Indians hold the famous first Thanksgiving feast in colonial America.

1623—Colonization of New Hampshire is begun by the English.

1624—Colonization of present-day New York State is begun by the Dutch at Fort Orange (Albany).

1625—The Dutch start building New Amsterdam (now New York City).

1630—The town of Boston, Massachusetts, is founded by the English Puritans.

1633—Colonization of Connecticut is begun by the English.

1634—Colonization of Maryland is begun by the English.

1636—Harvard, the colonies' first college, is founded in Massachusetts. Rhode Island colonization begins when Englishman Roger Williams founds Providence.

1638—Delaware colonization begins as Swedes build Fort Christina at present-day Wilmington.

1640—Stephen Daye of Cambridge, Massachusetts prints *The Bay Psalm Book*, the first English-language book published in what is now the U.S.

1643—Swedish settlers begin colonizing Pennsylvania.

About 1650—North Carolina is colonized by Virginia settlers.

1660—New Jersey colonization is begun by the Dutch at present-day Jersey City.

1670—South Carolina colonization is begun by the English near Charleston.

1673—Jacques Marquette and Louis Jolliet explore the upper Mississippi River for France.

1682 — Philadelphia, Pennsylvania, is settled. La Salle explores Mississippi River all the way to its mouth in Louisiana and claims the whole Mississippi Valley for France.

1693 — College of William and Mary is founded in Williamsburg, Virginia.

1700 — Colonial population is about 250,000.

1703 — Benjamin Franklin is born in Boston.

1732 — George Washington, first president of the U.S., is born in Westmoreland County, Virginia.

1733 — James Oglethorpe founds Savannah, Georgia; Georgia is established as the thirteenth colony.

1735 — John Adams, second president of the U.S., is born in Braintree, Massachusetts.

1737 — William Byrd founds Richmond, Virginia.

1738 — British troops are sent to Georgia over border dispute with Spain.

1739 — Black insurrection takes place in South Carolina.

1740 — English Parliament passes act allowing naturalization of immigrants to American colonies after seven-year residence.

1743 — Thomas Jefferson is born in Albemarle County, Virginia. Benjamin Franklin retires at age thirty-seven to devote himself to scientific inquiries and public service.

1744 — King George's War begins; France joins war effort against England.

1745 — During King George's War, France raids settlements in Maine and New York.

1747 — Classes begin at Princeton College in New Jersey.

1748 — The Treaty of Aix-la-Chapelle concludes King George's War.

1749 — Parliament legally recognizes slavery in colonies and the inauguration of the plantation system in the South. George Washington becomes the surveyor for Culpepper County in Virginia.

1750 — Thomas Walker passes through and names Cumberland Gap on his way toward Kentucky region. Colonial population is about 1,200,000.

1751 — James Madison, fourth president of the U.S., is born in Port Conway, Virginia. English Parliament passes Currency Act, banning New England colonies from issuing paper money. George Washington travels to Barbados.

1752 — Pennsylvania Hospital, the first general hospital in the colonies, is founded in Philadelphia. Benjamin Franklin uses a kite in a thunderstorm to demonstrate that lightning is a form of electricity.

1753 — George Washington delivers command that the French withdraw from the Ohio River Valley; French disregard the demand. Colonial population is about 1,328,000.

1754 — French and Indian War begins (extends to Europe as the Seven Years' War). Washington surrenders at Fort Necessity.

1755 — French and Indians ambush Braddock. Washington becomes commander of Virginia troops.

1756 — England declares war on France.

1758 — James Monroe, fifth president of the U.S., is born in Westmoreland County, Virginia.

1759 — Cherokee Indian war begins in southern colonies; hostilities extend to 1761. George Washington marries Martha Dandridge Custis.

1760 — George III becomes king of England. Colonial population is about 1,600,000.

1762 — England declares war on Spain.

1763 — Treaty of Paris concludes the French and Indian War and the Seven Years' War. England gains Canada and most other French lands east of the Mississippi River.

1764 — British pass the Sugar Act to gain tax money from the colonists. The issue of taxation without representation is first introduced in Boston. John Adams marries Abigail Smith.

1765 — Stamp Act goes into effect in the colonies. Business virtually stops as almost all colonists refuse to use the stamps.

1766 — British repeal the Stamp Act.

1767—John Quincy Adams, sixth president of the U.S. and son of second president John Adams, is born in Braintree, Massachusetts. Andrew Jackson, seventh president of the U.S., is born in Waxhaw settlement, South Carolina.

1769—Daniel Boone sights the Kentucky Territory.

1770—In the Boston Massacre, British soldiers kill five colonists and injure six. Townshend Acts are repealed, thus eliminating all duties on imports to the colonies except tea.

1771—Benjamin Franklin begins his autobiography, a work that he will never complete. The North Carolina assembly passes the "Bloody Act," which makes rioters guilty of treason.

1772—Samuel Adams rouses colonists to consider British threats to self-government.

1773—English Parliament passes the Tea Act. Colonists dressed as Mohawk Indians board British tea ships and toss 342 casks of tea into the water in what becomes known as the Boston Tea Party. William Henry Harrison is born in Charles City County, Virginia.

1774—British close the port of Boston to punish the city for the Boston Tea Party. First Continental Congress convenes in Philadelphia.

1775—American Revolution begins with battles of Lexington and Concord, Massachusetts. Second Continental Congress opens in Philadelphia. George Washington becomes commander-in-chief of the Continental army.

1776—Declaration of Independence is adopted on July 4.

1777—Congress adopts the American flag with thirteen stars and thirteen stripes. John Adams is sent to France to negotiate peace treaty.

1778—France declares war against Great Britain and becomes U.S. ally.

1779—British surrender to Americans at Vincennes. Thomas Jefferson is elected governor of Virginia. James Madison is elected to the Continental Congress.

1780—Benedict Arnold, first American traitor, defects to the British.

1781—Articles of Confederation go into effect. Cornwallis surrenders to George Washington at Yorktown, ending the American Revolution.

1782—American commissioners, including John Adams, sign peace treaty with British in Paris. Thomas Jefferson's wife, Martha, dies. Martin Van Buren is born in Kinderhook, New York.

1784—Zachary Taylor is born near Barboursville, Virginia.

1785—Congress adopts the dollar as the unit of currency. John Adams is made minister to Great Britain. Thomas Jefferson is appointed minister to France.

1786—Shays's Rebellion begins in Massachusetts.

1787—Constitutional Convention assembles in Philadelphia, with George Washington presiding; U.S. Constitution is adopted. Delaware, New Jersey, and Pennsylvania become states.

1788—Virginia, South Carolina, New York, Connecticut, New Hampshire, Maryland, and Massachusetts become states. U.S. Constitution is ratified. New York City is declared U.S. capital.

1789—Presidential electors elect George Washington and John Adams as first president and vice-president. Thomas Jefferson is appointed secretary of state. North Carolina becomes a state. French Revolution begins.

1790—Supreme Court meets for the first time. Rhode Island becomes a state. First national census in the U.S. counts 3,929,214 persons. John Tyler is born in Charles City County, Virginia.

1791—Vermont enters the Union. U.S. Bill of Rights, the first ten amendments to the Constitution, goes into effect. District of Columbia is established. James Buchanan is born in Stony Batter, Pennsylvania.

1792—Thomas Paine publishes *The Rights of Man*. Kentucky becomes a state. Two political parties are formed in the U.S., Federalist and Republican. Washington is elected to a second term, with Adams as vice-president.

1793—War between France and Britain begins; U.S. declares neutrality. Eli Whitney invents the cotton gin; cotton production and slave labor increase in the South.

1794—Eleventh Amendment to the Constitution is passed, limiting federal courts' power. "Whiskey Rebellion" in Pennsylvania protests federal whiskey tax. James Madison marries Dolley Payne Todd.

1795—George Washington signs the Jay Treaty with Great Britain. Treaty of San Lorenzo, between U.S. and Spain, settles Florida boundary and gives U.S. right to navigate the Mississippi. James Polk is born near Pineville, North Carolina.

1796—Tennessee enters the Union. Washington gives his Farewell Address, refusing a third presidential term. John Adams is elected president and Thomas Jefferson vice-president.

1797—Adams recommends defense measures against possible war with France. Napoleon Bonaparte and his army march against Austrians in Italy. U.S. population is about 4,900,000.

1798—Washington is named commander-in-chief of the U.S. Army. Department of the Navy is created. Alien and Sedition Acts are passed. Napoleon's troops invade Egypt and Switzerland.

1799—George Washington dies at Mount Vernon, New York. James Monroe is elected governor of Virginia. French Revolution ends. Napoleon becomes ruler of France.

1800—Thomas Jefferson and Aaron Burr tie for president. U.S. capital is moved from Philadelphia to Washington, D.C. The White House is built as presidents' home. Spain returns Louisiana to France. Millard Fillmore is born in Locke, New York.

1801—After thirty-six ballots, House of Representatives elects Thomas Jefferson president, making Burr vice-president. James Madison is named secretary of state.

1802—Congress abolishes excise taxes. U.S. Military Academy is founded at West Point, New York.

1803—Ohio enters the Union. Louisiana Purchase treaty is signed with France, greatly expanding U.S. territory.

1804—Twelfth Amendment to the Constitution rules that president and vice-president be elected separately. Alexander Hamilton is killed by Vice-President Aaron Burr in a duel. Orleans Territory is established. Napoleon crowns himself emperor of France. Franklin Pierce is born in Hillsborough Lower Village, New Hampshire.

1805—Thomas Jefferson begins his second term as president. Lewis and Clark expedition reaches the Pacific Ocean.

1806—Coinage of silver dollars is stopped; resumes in 1836.

1807—Aaron Burr is acquitted in treason trial. Embargo Act closes U.S. ports to trade.

1808—James Madison is elected president. Congress outlaws importing slaves from Africa. Andrew Johnson is born in Raleigh, North Carolina.

1809—Abraham Lincoln is born near Hodgenville, Kentucky.

1810—U.S. population is 7,240,000.

1811—William Henry Harrison defeats Indians at Tippecanoe. Monroe is named secretary of state.

1812—Louisiana becomes a state. U.S. declares war on Britain (War of 1812). James Madison is reelected president. Napoleon invades Russia.

1813—British forces take Fort Niagara and Buffalo, New York.

1814—Francis Scott Key writes "The Star-Spangled Banner." British troops burn much of Washington, D.C., including the White House. Treaty of Ghent ends War of 1812. James Monroe becomes secretary of war.

1815—Napoleon meets his final defeat at Battle of Waterloo.

1816—James Monroe is elected president. Indiana becomes a state.

1817—Mississippi becomes a state. Construction on Erie Canal begins.

1818—Illinois enters the Union. The present thirteen-stripe flag is adopted. Border between U.S. and Canada is agreed upon.

1819—Alabama becomes a state. U.S. purchases Florida from Spain. Thomas Jefferson establishes the University of Virginia.

1820—James Monroe is reelected. In the Missouri Compromise, Maine enters the Union as a free (non-slave) state.

1821—Missouri enters the Union as a slave state. Santa Fe Trail opens the American Southwest. Mexico declares independence from Spain. Napoleon Bonaparte dies.

1822—U.S. recognizes Mexico and Colombia. Liberia in Africa is founded as a home for freed slaves. Ulysses S. Grant is born in Point Pleasant, Ohio. Rutherford B. Hayes is born in Delaware, Ohio.

1823—Monroe Doctrine closes North and South America to European colonizing or invasion.

1824—House of Representatives elects John Quincy Adams president when none of the four candidates wins a majority in national election. Mexico becomes a republic.

1825—Erie Canal is opened. U.S. population is 11,300,000.

1826—Thomas Jefferson and John Adams both die on July 4, the fiftieth anniversary of the Declaration of Independence.

1828—Andrew Jackson is elected president. Tariff of Abominations is passed, cutting imports.

1829—James Madison attends Virginia's constitutional convention. Slavery is abolished in Mexico. Chester A. Arthur is born in Fairfield, Vermont.

1830—Indian Removal Act to resettle Indians west of the Mississippi is approved.

1831—James Monroe dies in New York City. James A. Garfield is born in Orange, Ohio. Cyrus McCormick develops his reaper.

1832—Andrew Jackson, nominated by the new Democratic Party, is reelected president.

1833—Britain abolishes slavery in its colonies. Benjamin Harrison is born in North Bend, Ohio.

1835—Federal government becomes debt-free for the first time.

1836—Martin Van Buren becomes president. Texas wins independence from Mexico. Arkansas joins the Union. James Madison dies at Montpelier, Virginia.

1837—Michigan enters the Union. U.S. population is 15,900,000. Grover Cleveland is born in Caldwell, New Jersey.

1840—William Henry Harrison is elected president.

1841—President Harrison dies in Washington, D.C., one month after inauguration. Vice-President John Tyler succeeds him.

1843—William McKinley is born in Niles, Ohio.

1844—James Knox Polk is elected president. Samuel Morse sends first telegraphic message.

1845—Texas and Florida become states. Potato famine in Ireland causes massive emigration from Ireland to U.S. Andrew Jackson dies near Nashville, Tennessee.

1846—Iowa enters the Union. War with Mexico begins.

1847—U.S. captures Mexico City.

1848—John Quincy Adams dies in Washington, D.C. Zachary Taylor becomes president. Treaty of Guadalupe Hidalgo ends Mexico-U.S. war. Wisconsin becomes a state.

1849—James Polk dies in Nashville, Tennessee.

1850—President Taylor dies in Washington, D.C.; Vice-President Millard Fillmore succeeds him. California enters the Union, breaking tie between slave and free states.

1852—Franklin Pierce is elected president.

1853—Gadsden Purchase transfers Mexican territory to U.S.

1854—"War for Bleeding Kansas" is fought between slave and free states.

1855—Czar Nicholas I of Russia dies, succeeded by Alexander II.

1856—James Buchanan is elected president. In Massacre of Potawatomi Creek, Kansas-slavers are murdered by free-staters. Woodrow Wilson is born in Staunton, Virginia.

1857—William Howard Taft is born in Cincinnati, Ohio.

1858—Minnesota enters the Union. Theodore Roosevelt is born in New York City.

1859—Oregon becomes a state.

1860—Abraham Lincoln is elected president; South Carolina secedes from the Union in protest.

1861—Arkansas, Tennessee, North Carolina, and Virginia secede. Kansas enters the Union as a free state. Civil War begins.

1862—Union forces capture Fort Henry, Roanoke Island, Fort Donelson, Jacksonville, and New Orleans; Union armies are defeated at the battles of Bull Run and Fredericksburg. Martin Van Buren dies in Kinderhook, New York. John Tyler dies near Charles City, Virginia.

1863—Lincoln issues Emancipation Proclamation: all slaves held in rebelling territories are declared free. West Virginia becomes a state.

1864—Abraham Lincoln is reelected. Nevada becomes a state.

1865—Lincoln is assassinated in Washington, D.C., and succeeded by Andrew Johnson. U.S. Civil War ends on May 26. Thirteenth Amendment abolishes slavery. Warren G. Harding is born in Blooming Grove, Ohio.

1867—Nebraska becomes a state. U.S. buys Alaska from Russia for $7,200,000. Reconstruction Acts are passed.

1868—President Johnson is impeached for violating Tenure of Office Act, but is acquitted by Senate. Ulysses S. Grant is elected president. Fourteenth Amendment prohibits voting discrimination. James Buchanan dies in Lancaster, Pennsylvania.

1869—Franklin Pierce dies in Concord, New Hampshire.

1870—Fifteenth Amendment gives blacks the right to vote.

1872—Grant is reelected over Horace Greeley. General Amnesty Act pardons ex-Confederates. Calvin Coolidge is born in Plymouth Notch, Vermont.

1874—Millard Fillmore dies in Buffalo, New York. Herbert Hoover is born in West Branch, Iowa.

1875—Andrew Johnson dies in Carter's Station, Tennessee.

1876—Colorado enters the Union. "Custer's last stand": he and his men are massacred by Sioux Indians at Little Big Horn, Montana.

1877—Rutherford B. Hayes is elected president as all disputed votes are awarded to him.

1880—James A. Garfield is elected president.

1881—President Garfield is assassinated and dies in Elberon, New Jersey. Vice-President Chester A. Arthur succeeds him.

1882—U.S. bans Chinese immigration. Franklin D. Roosevelt is born in Hyde Park, New York.

1884—Grover Cleveland is elected president. Harry S. Truman is born in Lamar, Missouri.

1885—Ulysses S. Grant dies in Mount McGregor, New York.

1886—Statue of Liberty is dedicated. Chester A. Arthur dies in New York City.

1888—Benjamin Harrison is elected president.

1889—North Dakota, South Dakota, Washington, and Montana become states.

1890—Dwight D. Eisenhower is born in Denison, Texas. Idaho and Wyoming become states.

1892—Grover Cleveland is elected president.

1893—Rutherford B. Hayes dies in Fremont, Ohio.

1896—William McKinley is elected president. Utah becomes a state.

1898—U.S. declares war on Spain over Cuba.

1900—McKinley is reelected. Boxer Rebellion against foreigners in China begins.

1901—McKinley is assassinated by anarchist Leon Czolgosz in Buffalo, New York; Theodore Roosevelt becomes president. Benjamin Harrison dies in Indianapolis, Indiana.

1902—U.S. acquires perpetual control over Panama Canal.

1903—Alaskan frontier is settled.

1904—Russian-Japanese War breaks out. Theodore Roosevelt wins presidential election.

1905—Treaty of Portsmouth signed, ending Russian-Japanese War.

1906—U.S. troops occupy Cuba.

1907—President Roosevelt bars all Japanese immigration. Oklahoma enters the Union.

1908—William Howard Taft becomes president. Grover Cleveland dies in Princeton, New Jersey. Lyndon B. Johnson is born near Stonewall, Texas.

1909—NAACP is founded under W.E.B. DuBois

1910—China abolishes slavery.

1911—Chinese Revolution begins. Ronald Reagan is born in Tampico, Illinois.

1912—Woodrow Wilson is elected president. Arizona and New Mexico become states.

1913—Federal income tax is introduced in U.S. through the Sixteenth Amendment. Richard Nixon is born in Yorba Linda, California. Gerald Ford is born in Omaha, Nebraska.

1914—World War I begins.

1915—British liner *Lusitania* is sunk by German submarine.

1916—Wilson is reelected president.

1917—U.S. breaks diplomatic relations with Germany. Czar Nicholas of Russia abdicates as revolution begins. U.S. declares war on Austria-Hungary. John F. Kennedy is born in Brookline, Massachusetts.

1918—Wilson proclaims "Fourteen Points" as war aims. On November 11, armistice is signed between Allies and Germany.

1919—Eighteenth Amendment prohibits sale and manufacture of intoxicating liquors. Wilson presides over first League of Nations; wins Nobel Peace Prize. Theodore Roosevelt dies in Oyster Bay, New York.

1920—Nineteenth Amendment (women's suffrage) is passed. Warren Harding is elected president.

1921—Adolf Hitler's stormtroopers begin to terrorize political opponents.

1922—Irish Free State is established. Soviet states form USSR. Benito Mussolini forms Fascist government in Italy.

1923—President Harding dies in San Francisco, California; he is succeeded by Vice-President Calvin Coolidge.

1924—Coolidge is elected president. Woodrow Wilson dies in Washington, D.C. James Carter is born in Plains, Georgia. George Bush is born in Milton, Massachusetts.

1925—Hitler reorganizes Nazi Party and publishes first volume of *Mein Kampf.*

1926—Fascist youth organizations founded in Germany and Italy. Republic of Lebanon proclaimed.

1927—Stalin becomes Soviet dictator. Economic conference in Geneva attended by fifty-two nations.

1928—Herbert Hoover is elected president. U.S. and many other nations sign Kellogg-Briand pacts to outlaw war.

1929—Stock prices in New York crash on "Black Thursday"; the Great Depression begins.

1930—Bank of U.S. and its many branches close (most significant bank failure of the year). William Howard Taft dies in Washington, D.C.

1931—Emigration from U.S. exceeds immigration for first time as Depression deepens.

1932—Franklin D. Roosevelt wins presidential election in a Democratic landslide.

1933—First concentration camps are erected in Germany. U.S. recognizes USSR and resumes trade. Twenty-First Amendment repeals prohibition. Calvin Coolidge dies in Northampton, Massachusetts.

1934—Severe dust storms hit Plains states. President Roosevelt passes U.S. Social Security Act.

1936—Roosevelt is reelected. Spanish Civil War begins. Hitler and Mussolini form Rome-Berlin Axis.

1937—Roosevelt signs Neutrality Act.

1938—Roosevelt sends appeal to Hitler and Mussolini to settle European problems amicably.

1939—Germany takes over Czechoslovakia and invades Poland, starting World War II.

1940—Roosevelt is reelected for a third term.

1941—Japan bombs Pearl Harbor, U.S. declares war on Japan. Germany and Italy declare war on U.S.; U.S. then declares war on them.

1942—Allies agree not to make separate peace treaties with the enemies. U.S. government transfers more than 100,000 Nisei (Japanese-Americans) from west coast to inland concentration camps.

1943—Allied bombings of Germany begin.

1944—Roosevelt is reelected for a fourth term. Allied forces invade Normandy on D-Day.

1945—President Franklin D. Roosevelt dies in Warm Springs, Georgia; Vice-President Harry S. Truman succeeds him. Mussolini is killed; Hitler commits suicide. Germany surrenders. U.S. drops atomic bomb on Hiroshima; Japan surrenders: end of World War II.

1946—U.N. General Assembly holds its first session in London. Peace conference of twenty-one nations is held in Paris.

1947—Peace treaties are signed in Paris. "Cold War" is in full swing.

1948—U.S. passes Marshall Plan Act, providing $17 billion in aid for Europe. U.S. recognizes new nation of Israel. India and Pakistan become free of British rule. Truman is elected president.

1949—Republic of Eire is proclaimed in Dublin. Russia blocks land route access from Western Germany to Berlin; airlift begins. U.S., France, and Britain agree to merge their zones of occupation in West Germany. Apartheid program begins in South Africa.

1950—Riots in Johannesburg, South Africa, against apartheid. North Korea invades South Korea. U.N. forces land in South Korea and recapture Seoul.

1951—Twenty-Second Amendment limits president to two terms.

1952—Dwight D. Eisenhower resigns as supreme commander in Europe and is elected president.

1953—Stalin dies; struggle for power in Russia follows. Rosenbergs are executed for espionage.

1954—U.S. and Japan sign mutual defense agreement.

1955—Blacks in Montgomery, Alabama, boycott segregated bus lines.

1956—Eisenhower is reelected president. Soviet troops march into Hungary.

1957—U.S. agrees to withdraw ground forces from Japan. Russia launches first satellite, *Sputnik*.

1958—European Common Market comes into being. Fidel Castro begins war against Batista government in Cuba.

1959—Alaska becomes the forty-ninth state. Hawaii becomes fiftieth state. Castro becomes premier of Cuba. De Gaulle is proclaimed president of the Fifth Republic of France.

1960—Historic debates between Senator John F. Kennedy and Vice-President Richard Nixon are televised. Kennedy is elected president. Brezhnev becomes president of USSR.

1961—Berlin Wall is constructed. Kennedy and Khrushchev confer in Vienna. In Bay of Pigs incident, Cubans trained by CIA attempt to overthrow Castro.

1962—U.S. military council is established in South Vietnam.

1963—Riots and beatings by police and whites mark civil rights demonstrations in Birmingham, Alabama; 30,000 troops are called out, Martin Luther King, Jr., is arrested. Freedom marchers descend on Washington, D.C., to demonstrate. President Kennedy is assassinated in Dallas, Texas; Vice-President Lyndon B. Johnson is sworn in as president.

1964—U.S. aircraft bomb North Vietnam. Johnson is elected president. Herbert Hoover dies in New York City.

1965—U.S. combat troops arrive in South Vietnam.

1966—Thousands protest U.S. policy in Vietnam. National Guard quells race riots in Chicago.

1967—Six-Day War between Israel and Arab nations.

1968—Martin Luther King, Jr., is assassinated in Memphis, Tennessee. Senator Robert Kennedy is assassinated in Los Angeles. Riots and police brutality take place at Democratic National Convention in Chicago. Richard Nixon is elected president. Czechoslovakia is invaded by Soviet troops.

1969—Dwight D. Eisenhower dies in Washington, D.C. Hundreds of thousands of people in several U.S. cities demonstrate against Vietnam War.

1970—Four Vietnam War protesters are killed by National Guardsmen at Kent State University in Ohio.

1971—Twenty-Sixth Amendment allows eighteen-year-olds to vote.

1972—Nixon visits Communist China; is reelected president in near-record landslide. Watergate affair begins when five men are arrested in the Watergate hotel complex in Washington, D.C. Nixon announces resignations of aides Haldeman, Ehrlichman, and Dean and Attorney General Kleindienst as a result of Watergate-related charges. Harry S. Truman dies in Kansas City, Missouri.

1973—Vice-President Spiro Agnew resigns; Gerald Ford is named vice-president. Vietnam peace treaty is formally approved after nineteen months of negotiations. Lyndon B. Johnson dies in San Antonio, Texas.

1974—As a result of Watergate cover-up, impeachment is considered; Nixon resigns and Ford becomes president. Ford pardons Nixon and grants limited amnesty to Vietnam War draft evaders and military deserters.

1975—U.S. civilians are evacuated from Saigon, South Vietnam, as Communist forces complete takeover of South Vietnam.

1976—U.S. celebrates its Bicentennial. James Earl Carter becomes president.

1977—Carter pardons most Vietnam draft evaders, numbering some 10,000.

1980—Ronald Reagan is elected president.

1981—President Reagan is shot in the chest in assassination attempt. Sandra Day O'Connor is appointed first woman justice of the Supreme Court.

1983—U.S. troops invade island of Grenada.

1984—Reagan is reelected president. Democratic candidate Walter Mondale's running mate, Geraldine Ferraro, is the first woman selected for vice-president by a major U.S. political party.

1985—Soviet Communist Party secretary Konstantin Chernenko dies; Mikhail Gorbachev succeeds him. U.S. and Soviet officials discuss arms control in Geneva. Reagan and Gorbachev hold summit conference in Geneva. Racial tensions accelerate in South Africa.

1986—Space shuttle *Challenger* explodes shortly after takeoff; crew of seven dies. U.S. bombs bases in Libya. Corazon Aquino defeats Ferdinand Marcos in Philippine presidential election.

1987—Iraqi missile rips the U.S. frigate *Stark* in the Persian Gulf, killing thirty-seven American sailors. Congress holds hearings to investigate sale of U.S. arms to Iran to finance Nicaraguan *contra* movement.

1988—President Reagan and Soviet leader Gorbachev sign INF treaty, eliminating intermediate nuclear forces. Severe drought sweeps the United States. George Bush is elected president.

1989—East Germany opens Berlin Wall, allowing citizens free exit. Communists lose control of governments in Poland, Romania, and Czechoslovakia. Chinese troops massacre over 1,000 prodemocracy student demonstrators in Beijing's Tiananmen Square.

1990—Iraq annexes Kuwait, provoking the threat of war. East and West Germany are reunited. The Cold War between the United States and the Soviet Union comes to a close. Several Soviet republics make moves toward independence.

1991—Backed by a coalition of members of the United Nations, U.S. troops drive Iraqis from Kuwait. Latvia, Lithuania, and Estonia withdraw from the USSR. The Soviet Union dissolves as its republics secede to form a Commonwealth of Independent States.

1992—U.N. forces fail to stop fighting in territories of former Yugoslavia. More than fifty people are killed and more than six hundred buildings burned in rioting in Los Angeles. U.S. unemployment reaches eight-year high. Hurricane Andrew devastates southern Florida and parts of Louisiana. International relief supplies and troops are sent to combat famine and violence in Somalia.

1993—U.S.-led forces use airplanes and missiles to attack military targets in Iraq. William Jefferson Clinton becomes the forty-second U.S. president.

1994—Richard M. Nixon dies in New York City.

Index

Page numbers in boldface type indicate illustrations.

About the Author

Paul P. Sipiera is a professor of physical sciences and the director of the Center for Meteorite and Planetary Studies at William Rainey Harper College in Palatine, Illinois. He is also a research associate in geology at the Field Museum of Natural History in Chicago. As a member of the National Science Foundation's Antarctic Research Program, he has studied geological features of the icy continent. A teacher of astronomy and geology, his specialties are meteorites, moon rocks, and volcanoes. In his spare time Mr. Sipiera gardens, grows vegetables, and cuts wood on his farm in Galena, Illinois.